# Whispers
## TO THE
# Weary

Resting in God's Love and the Finished Work of Jesus—in the midst of burnout, grief, and shame.

## A 30-DAY DEVOTIONAL OF POEMS AND REFLECTIONS

Claire Staton

**Whispers to the Weary**
© 2025 **Claire Staton**
All rights reserved.

ISBN: **978-1-960862-03-7**

**Cover Design & Interior Layout:** Designed by Jana Linville
**Published by:** Claire Staton
Printed in the United States of America

**Scripture References:** Unless otherwise noted, Scripture quotations are from the **Holy Bible, New International Version®, NIV®**. Copyright © 1973, 1978, 1984, 2011 by **Biblica, Inc.** Used by permission. All rights reserved worldwide.

For permissions, inquiries, or more information, visit: PowerOfJesusInTheEveryDay.com

# Acknowledgments

Writing this book has been a journey of both surrender and grace, and I could not have done it alone.

To **Jonathan**—Thank you for being a place where my voice was welcomed, strengthened, and celebrated. Where I could process the hard and the hopeful, and never feel rushed or silenced. Your love, patience, and steady belief have been an anchor for me. I love everything about you—your steady heart, your quiet strength, your forgiving heart, your joy. I love how God gave me you to complement me so beautifully —meeting my weaknesses with your strength, my questions with your peace. I'm endlessly grateful to walk through this life with you.

To my **sweet children**—you are beautiful reminders of God's goodness. Your joy, curiosity, and laughter fill my heart. I am unbelievably proud of who God made you to be. You have taught me what it means to love fully, live in the moment, and trust God with the unknown. I pray you continue to know how deeply loved you are by Jesus.

To **our family**—thank you for your encouragement, for always cheering me on, your continual prayers, and your constant reminders that God is always faithful. You have been His hands and feet to me and my family in moments when we needed it most and ones we didn't even know we needed.

To my **friends and community**—who have spoken life over this project, encouraged me when I doubted, and reminded me why these words matter—thank you for believing in the message of this book and in the God who whispers to the weary.

To **those who have walked with me** through seasons of grief, struggle, and deep surrender—you have shown me what it means to live in light of the gospel. Your love and faithfulness have been a reflection of Christ in my life.

To my **designer, Jana**—thank you for helping bring this book to life with excellence and care.

And most of all, to **Jesus**—every word in this book is because of You. You are the One who turns ashes into beauty (Isaiah 61:3 NIV), who speaks peace into the chaos, and who whispers truth in the midst of our weariness. This book is just a small reflection of the love and grace You have poured into my life. May it glorify You alone.

To **every reader**—thank you for opening these pages. My prayer is that these words meet you where you are and lead you deeper into the rest, love, and presence of Christ.

With much gratitude,

*Claire Staton*

# Hello There, Dear Reader,

This collection of poems and reflections isn't just a book; it's an invitation into a journey. A journey of wrestling, questioning, and ultimately resting in the grace and truth of the gospel (the good news of Jesus). Each poem was born out of raw, unfiltered moments—moments of joy, pain, and everything in between. These words became my prayers when I had no others, my way of making sense of the chaos and beauty that life so often brings.

I didn't set out to write a devotional. I set out to write down pieces of my heart. In doing so, I realized how much of my story mirrors the stories of others: striving to measure up, searching for who I really am, wrestling with fear, and longing for rest. Through every page, my hope is that you will see not just my story, but your own, and most importantly, how God meets us in the messy middle with such tender grace and truth.

Life often feels like a whirlwind, doesn't it? The demands, the distractions, the deep desire to just be enough. It's easy to forget the beautiful truth: we were never meant to carry it all alone. We have a Savior who carried it for us—who whispers to our weary hearts, "Come to me, all you who are weary and burdened, and I will give you rest (Matthew 11:28 NIV)."

But how often do we listen to a different voice? The enemy screamed lies at me for years:

- *The lie that I wasn't worthy of love left me isolated and self-focused.*
- *The lie that I had to achieve more, be more, and do more to be valuable left me empty and burnt out.*
- *The lie that I was responsible for others' happiness crushed me under a weight I was never meant to bear.*

Yet the gospel silences those lies.

- **My worth isn't earned; it's given by Jesus.**

- **My identity isn't fragile; it's secured in Jesus.**
- **The weight of saving others isn't mine to carry; it's Jesus', their Savior.**

This devotional isn't about perfect answers or polished faith. It's about the kind of faith that grows in the trenches of real life—the kind of faith that clings to the cross when nothing else makes sense. Whether you're overflowing with gratitude or barely hanging on, my prayer is that these poems and reflections will draw you closer to the One who loves you more than you can imagine.

Take your time with these pages. Sit with them. Reflect, pray, and let the Spirit whisper to you in the quiet moments. Let the words point you back to our Creator who knows you, sees you, and calls you His own.

Through His finished work on the cross, Jesus calls us into rest—freedom from fear, striving, and shame. This is not a journey of achieving or performing, but of surrendering. The freedom He gives allows us to live as the people God created us to be, with hearts that are whole and at peace.

So, as you read, I pray that you'll lay down the burdens you were never meant to carry. I pray you'll hear the whispers of His truth above the noise, and you'll choose to enter into the rest only God can provide. My deepest desire is that as you journey through this devotional, you'll find rest for your soul and a renewed sense of wonder at the wholeness of walking in His grace.

With much love and prayer,

# The Power of Jesus in the Everyday

The gospel is the good news that Jesus Christ, the Son of God, came to rescue us from sin and death. He lived the perfect life we could never live, died the death we deserved, and rose again, conquering sin and death. Through His finished work on the cross, we are not just forgiven—we are made new. We are brought from death to life, from striving to rest, from shame to freedom.

But the gospel isn't just a message we believe once—**it's the truth we need every single day**. It meets us in our struggles, in our insecurities, in the places we feel most unworthy, and reminds us of who we are in Christ.

When rejection stings, the gospel reminds us, "Jesus chose you."

Maybe you didn't get invited. Maybe you weren't picked for the promotion. Maybe someone you loved walked away. But Jesus? He saw you at your worst and still said, You are mine (John 15:16 NIV). His love isn't based on what you bring to the table; it is steadfast, unchanging, and secure.

When betrayal cuts deep, the gospel reminds us, "We once betrayed Jesus, but He still chose us."

Friends fail. Family wounds. People let us down. But before we ever felt the sting of betrayal, Jesus endured it first. Judas sold Him out, Peter denied Him, and the crowds demanded His death in place of the release of a murderer, Barabbas—yet He still endured the cross – for the joy of what it would bring (Hebrews 12:2 NIV). His love isn't conditional; it's sacrificial. Even when we are unfaithful, He remains faithful (2 Timothy 2:13 NIV).

When we feel purposeless, the gospel reminds us, "You were created for a mission."

Sometimes it's easy to feel like you don't matter, like your life isn't making a difference. But before you took your first breath, God had a purpose for you specifically (Ephesians 2:10 NIV). You were made to reflect His glory, to bring His light into dark places, to love the people around you in His name. Your worth isn't tied to what you accomplish—it's secured in who God is.

When shame creeps in, the gospel reminds us, "You are fully forgiven."

The enemy loves to remind us of our past. Maybe you've made mistakes that haunt you. Maybe you feel unworthy of love, of grace, of a fresh start. But the cross has the final word. It is finished (John 19:30 NIV). Jesus took your shame, your sin, and your guilt so you could stand before God blameless. You are not your worst moments. You are redeemed.

When anxiety and fear overwhelm, the gospel reminds us, "You are safe in His hands."

Life is unpredictable. The weight of "what ifs" can feel unbearable. But Jesus, the One who spoke the stars into existence, holds you in His hands (John 10:28-29 NIV). Nothing—not hardship, not loss, not even death—can separate you from His love (Romans 8:38-39 NIV). You don't have to control everything because He is already in control.

When exhaustion and burnout hit, the gospel reminds us to, "Come to Jesus, and He will give you rest."

Maybe you're weary from always trying to be enough. Maybe you're tired of holding it all together. Jesus says, You were never meant to carry this alone (Matthew 11:28 NIV). His grace is sufficient. His strength is made perfect in your weakness. The pressure is off.

When loneliness lingers, the gospel assures, "You are seen and deeply loved."

You might feel overlooked. Forgotten. Like no one really sees the real you. But God does. He sees every tear, every unspoken ache, every hope hidden in your heart. You are not invisible to Him. He is near to the brokenhearted (Psalm 34:18 NIV).

But how can we be sure of this?

Because Jesus took our place.

Sin separated us from God—forever. The penalty for sin isn't just a bad life; it's death (Romans 6:23 NIV). Not just physical death, but eternal separation from God. That's hell.

But Jesus stepped in.

On the cross, He didn't just endure excruciating physical pain—He took on our sin and experienced separation from God for the first and only time in all eternity. That is the deepest agony possible. The very presence of God that had always been with Him—gone. And He did it for us so that we would never have to know eternal separation.

Jesus paid our debt so we could be made right with God. His sacrifice tore down the barrier of sin that stood between us and the Father, giving us access to His presence, both now and forever in heaven. Because of Him, we don't just have forgiveness—we have a restored relationship with God.

And that changes everything.

The gospel isn't just a distant theological concept—it's our daily lifeline. It speaks into every wound, every fear, every insecurity, and every failure. It reminds us that we don't have to fight for a place, because God invited us into His family. It tells us that we are not defined by our struggles, but by His victory.

So each day, preach the gospel to yourself. Let it shape your thoughts, direct your heart, and redefine how you respond to life's struggles. Jesus has already won the victory—walk in the freedom He died to give you.

## Preparing Your Heart for This Devotional

**Before you begin this journey, take a deep breath.**
Slow down. Let the rush of your day fade into the background for a moment.

This devotional isn't just something to read—it's an invitation. An invitation to step away from the noise, to sit in God's presence, and to listen. To hear **His whispers** above the chaos, above the striving, above the distractions that so easily pull our hearts away.

"The Lord said, 'Go out and stand on the mountain in the presence of the Lord, for the Lord is about to pass by.' Then a great and powerful wind tore the mountains apart and shattered the rocks before the Lord, but the Lord was not in the wind. After the wind there was an earthquake, but the Lord was not in the earthquake. After the earthquake came a fire, but the Lord was not in the fire. And after the fire came a gentle whisper." — 1 Kings 19:11-12 NIV

God wasn't in the wind, the earthquake, or the fire. **He was in the whisper.**

So before you turn the page, pause. Ask God to still your heart, to quiet the noise, to cover you in His love. Ask Him to make you ready—to hear, to receive, to rest in what He is speaking over you.

Each day begins with a raw, unfiltered poem—a reflection of real emotions, real struggles, real longing. Maybe you'll find your own heart reflected in the words. Maybe they will give voice to things you didn't even realize you were feeling.

But don't stop there.

**Grace in Focus** is where the power of the Gospel meets us—right where we are. It's one thing to hear about God's love, His peace, and His promises. It's another to let them **settle deep**, to **transform the way we think, live, and rest.**

After Grace in Focus, you'll find **A Moment with God and Your Heart's Response** sections—a special space where the Lord invites you to delight in Him and simply spend time with Him. Let it be a moment of acknowledging and honoring all of who He is, a place where your heart responds to His nearness.

Then comes **Ponder with Jesus**—a time of reflection guided by gentle but searching questions. I encourage you to sit with these questions, not rushing past them. Invite God to search you and reveal what needs to be revealed. Trust that He knows you better than anyone—better than you know yourself—because He made you.

Let this be more than reading.
Let it be an encounter with Jesus.
Let His whispers shape your heart.

## A Simple Prayer Before You Begin:

*"Father, search my heart. Remove distractions. Let me hear Your voice above all else. Open my eyes to Your truth—not just to know it, but to let it change me. Fill me with Your love so I can pour it out. Meet me in these pages and draw me closer to You. Amen."*

**Bring your whole self. Let His whispers find you. Let grace settle into the spaces you've been holding alone.**

# *Surrendering Control*

I grip so hard, afraid to let go,

Believing that losing control means I've failed.

I hold on until I am empty,

Until following You feels like obligation,

Until people feel like projects instead of souls to love.

Still, I cling.

But in Your patience, You gently ask me to loosen my grip,

Not all at once—just little by little.

You know that as I release, I will have more of You,

And less of me.

When the darkness creeps in, I freeze,

Familiar despair shouts its lies,

A relentless tug-of-war for my thoughts.

I want to hold on, to fix, to fight—

But You call me to trust.

Out of love, You open my eyes.

Even in the pain, You are in control.

You don't demand my strength—You desire my heart.

The only thing standing in the way is my pride.

I cannot do this without You holding me.

So instead of gripping so tightly,

I lift my hands in surrender—

Fully, joyfully, completely Yours.

## Grace in Focus

Control is a burden we were never meant to carry. Yet, we grip it tightly—our plans, our fears, even our faith—believing that if we just hold on hard enough, we can keep life from unraveling. But grief, suffering, and the unexpected have a way of showing us the truth: we were never in control to begin with. And that is good news.

The gospel offers us something far better than the illusion of control—it offers freedom. Jesus never called us to strive harder; He called us to trust deeper. **His invitation has never been, "Figure it all out," but He whispers "Come to Me, all who are weary and burdened, and I will give you rest"** (Matthew 11:28 NIV). On the cross, Jesus carried the ultimate burden—our sin, our shame, our striving—so we wouldn't have to. His grace is not just sufficient in our weakness (2 Corinthians 12:9 NIV); it is made perfect in it. When we surrender, we aren't losing—we're finally stepping into the peace and rest that only Jesus can give. We aren't giving up—we're giving in to the arms of a God who has always been faithful.

So maybe the hardest thing isn't letting go—maybe it's believing that we are fully held. Surrender is where true life begins. Let's open our hands, release our grip, and make room for God's power, grace, and love to do what only He can do.

## A Moment with God

Lord, I confess my desire to hold on to control. Teach me to trust You completely and surrender my heart to Your care. Thank You for the gospel—the good news that You lived the perfect life I couldn't live, died the death I deserved, and rose again to give me freedom and life forever lived with You in heaven. Because of this, I don't have to carry my burdens alone. In Jesus' name, Amen.

# Your Heart's Response

Take a moment to reflect on what you're holding on to too tightly. Write it down and pray over it, asking God to help you release it to Him. Meditate on Psalms 55:22, where Jesus invites you to lay your burdens at His feet.

# Ponder with Jesus

1. What is one thing you're holding on to that feels too heavy?

_____

_____

_____

_____

_____

_____

2. What is stopping you from letting God carry that burden for you?

_____

_____

_____

_____

_____

3. How might your life change if you fully surrendered it to Him?

_____

_____

_____

_____

_____

_____

# Freedom from Fear

You spoke so loudly—
Shouts of lies disguised as truth,
Telling me I was unseen, unworthy, never enough.
For too long, I listened.
For too long, I let you define me.
For too long, I lived as your prisoner.

But then, you bruised my Savior's heel...
But He crushed your head!

To what used to own me—
Fear, you have no hold.
Shame, you are silenced.
Striving, you have lost your grip.

Because in Jesus' victory, I AM FREE!

Free from fear—because I AM is greater.
Free from shame—because I AM calls me His own.
Free from striving—because I AM has clothed me in righteousness.
Free from doubt—because I AM knit me together with purpose.
Free to stand boldly—because I AM gives me strength.
Free to live fully—because I AM is the way, the truth, and the life.

## Grace in Focus

Fear is a thief. It sneaks in, wraps around our hearts, and screams the same old lies: You're not enough. You're unloved. You'll never measure up. It keeps us stuck, shrinking back when we were made to step forward. But Jesus whispers a better word. In Christ, we are fully known and fully loved—not in spite of our weaknesses, but right in the middle of them. Jesus' victory over sin and death means fear no longer has the final say. The enemy's lies have been silenced, crushed under the weight of the cross and the power of an empty tomb.

The truth is, we are not defined by fear—**we are defined by the power of the great I AM**. His perfect love casts out all fear (1 John 4:18 NIV), leaving no room for doubt, insecurity, or striving. Instead, He fills us with boldness, peace, and the unshakable assurance that we belong to Him. Fear may come knocking, but it no longer owns us. We are free.

## A Moment with God

Lord, thank You for the victory You've given me through Jesus. When fear tries to shout its lies, help me to stand firm in Your truth. Fill me with Your Spirit of power, love, and a sound mind (2 Timothy 1:7 NIV). In Jesus' name, Amen.

# Your Heart's Response

Write down one fear that has been holding you back. Find a scripture that speaks to God's promises and memorize it. When fear arises, speak that scripture aloud and remind yourself of Jesus' power over fear.

_____

_____

_____

_____

_____

_____

_____

_____

_____

_____

_____

_____

_____

_____

_____

_____

_____

_____

_____

_____

_____

# Ponder with Jesus

1. What is one fear you've been struggling with lately?

_____

_____

_____

_____

_____

_____

2. What do you think God is saying to you in the midst of that fear?

_____

_____

_____

_____

_____

_____

3. What would trusting God in this situation look like?

_____

_____

_____

_____

_____

_____

# Rest in Him

A gift I once overlooked,
Unaware of its worth,
Unaware of my need,
Unaware of how to receive it.

Rush. Strive. Hustle.
These were my rhythms, my anthem.
I chased productivity,
Neglecting the beauty of Your favor,
The grace woven into stillness.

But the gift of slowing down—
It awakens me to what truly matters.
To soak in Your presence,
To meditate on Your words,
To remember Your promises,
And to rest in the truth
That I am not God—but You are.

You are working when I am not.
I could meet with a hundred people,
But lifting them to You in prayer
Is infinitely more powerful.

Grief has been a teacher,
Slowing me to a humbler pace,
Revealing what my soul truly needs.
Yet even in my ignorance, You pursued me,
Patiently leading me to a better way.

There is no place like Your presence.
Peace and power intertwine,
A breath of stillness,
A spark of strength,
The motivation to move,
The permission to rest.

Thank You, Lord,
For calling me into Your rest—
Today, tomorrow, and forever.

## Grace in Focus

The world shouts, "Do more. Be more. Strive harder." It tells us that our worth is measured by our achievements, that rest is a luxury we can't afford. But the Holy Spirit whispers a different truth—one that silences the noise and invites us into something deeper: true rest. Because of Jesus' life, death, and resurrection, we don't have to hustle our way to God. Grace is not something we earn—it's a gift we receive. Jesus' finished work on the cross means we can stop striving and simply abide in His love (Ephesians 2:8–10 NIV). Resting in Christ isn't about doing nothing—it's about trusting in His sufficiency over our striving. It's about laying down the pressure to perform and leaning into His presence, His grace, His enough-ness. When we do, we find a peace the world can't give and a freedom only Jesus can provide. So today, take a breath. You don't have to prove yourself—you are already His.

## A Moment with God

Lord, thank You for the gift of rest. Thank You for the gospel, which reminds me that I don't have to strive to earn Your love—it's already mine because of Jesus' finished work. Help me to slow down, remember Your promises, and rest in Your presence. In Jesus' name, Amen.

# Your Heart's Response

Spend five minutes today in silence before God. Reflect on His sufficiency and allow yourself to simply rest in His presence. Meditate on Isaiah 43:1-2 NIV: "Do not fear, for I have redeemed you; I have summoned you by name; you are mine. When you pass through the waters, I will be with you; and when you pass through the rivers, they will not sweep over you.'" Ask God to cover you and fill you with His love.

# Ponder with Jesus

1. What is one area of your life where you feel constant pressure to perform?

_____

_____

_____

_____

_____

_____

2. Why do you think God rested after creating everything even though He didn't have to?

_____

_____

_____

_____

_____

_____

3. What is one way you can slow down and enjoy His presence today?

_____

_____

_____

_____

_____

_____

# Made for More

*"The people whom I formed for myself that they might declare my praise"*
(Isaiah 43:21 NIV)

Why am I here?
To chase happiness? To live for myself?
I tried. But it was never enough—always reaching, always empty.
So I turned to goodness, to striving, to being better.
Yet what I longed to do, I didn't. And what I swore I'd avoid, I ran toward.

I could never measure up—not even to my own standards.
How could I ever stand before a perfect Savior?
The ache inside me kept crying out,
Grasping at anything, worshiping the created instead of the Creator.
Each pursuit left me emptier, taking more than it ever gave.

But by Your grace, my eyes were opened.
I was made for You—to know You, to glorify You, to rest in You.
No pursuit has ever satisfied me like surrendering to You.
You alone are worthy.
You alone fill the gaps nothing else can.
Let my life be a song of praise, now and forever.

## Grace in Focus

This poem speaks to the ache we all carry—the longing for meaning, identity, and something greater than ourselves. Deep down, our hearts are searching for home, for purpose, for a love that truly satisfies. The gospel is God's answer to our longing. It tells us who we are and whose we are. We were created for Him, to know Him, to glorify Him, and to enjoy Him forever. No success, relationship, or earthly treasure can fill the void that only Jesus can. And yet, in the middle of our searching, He whispers to us. "Come to Me." "You are mine." "I have already made a way." On the cross, Jesus exchanged our brokenness for His righteousness (2 Corinthians 5:21 NIV). He took our sin, our shame, our wandering hearts and replaced them with grace, belonging, and purpose. He defeated sin and death so that nothing could stand between us and our Father ever again. We don't have to chase after meaning—we already have it in Him. Our purpose is simple, yet profound: to love Him, to enjoy Him, and to declare His goodness in all that we do. So today, if your soul is restless, lean in and listen. Jesus is whispering your name.

## A Moment with God

Lord, thank You for creating me for Your glory. Forgive me for chasing things that cannot satisfy and for worshiping your creation instead of You, our Creator. Thank You for the gospel, which shows me who I am in You—a beloved, chosen child with a purpose. In Jesus' name, Amen.

# Your Heart's Response

Take ten minutes to thank God for the ways He has uniquely made you to glorify Him. Reflect on how you can live out your purpose today.

_____

_____

_____

_____

_____

_____

_____

_____

_____

_____

_____

_____

_____

_____

_____

_____

_____

_____

_____

_____

_____

_____

_____

# Ponder with Jesus

1. What are you chasing that leaves you feeling empty?

_____

_____

_____

_____

_____

_____

2. What are three gifts that God has given you to share with the world?

_____

_____

_____

_____

_____

_____

3. What is one way you can live intentionally to point people to Jesus this
   week?

_____

_____

_____

_____

_____

_____

# *Found in Him*

You found me—dead, broken, and lost.
I wasn't looking for You. I was running toward everything but You.
Yet still, You chose me.

You opened my eyes to Your beauty,
Took my shattered pieces, and made me whole.
You gave me a new heart when I had nothing to offer.

You found me.
You had everything to lose, yet You laid it all down.
You took the wrath meant for me, so I could be restored to the Father.

Still, I wander. Still, I forget.
But even my running becomes a reminder of Your relentless love.
You never stop pursuing. You never stop saving.

You found me. And for that, I will never stop thanking You.

## Grace in Focus

This poem is a testimony of the gospel. It's the story of a God who steps into our brokenness, who breathes life into weary souls, who seeks us when we feel lost and calls us His own. Jesus didn't come for the perfect. He came for the hurting, the wandering, the ones who feel too far gone. And He didn't just call out from a distance—He came close. He bore the weight of our sin, took the punishment we deserved, and exchanged His righteousness for our shame. Not because we earned it, but because His love is relentless. And even now, in the moments we feel unworthy, in the silence of doubt and regret, He whispers: "I have called you by name. You are mine." "I chose you—not because of what you've done, but because of who I am." (Deuteronomy 7:7 NIV) "You are no longer defined by your failures, but by My sacrifice." The cross was not the end of the story. Jesus rose so we could rise with Him—made new, made whole, made His. We are no longer bound by our past, no longer searching for love we already have in Him. So today, let your soul lean in. Hear His whisper. Let grace do its work. You are chosen. You are loved. You are His.

## A Moment with God

Lord, thank You for finding me when I was lost and hopeless. Thank You for giving Your life to bring me into a relationship with God. Help me remember that my worth is not in what I do but in what You have done for me. Let my life reflect the gratitude I have for Your grace and mercy. In Jesus' name, Amen.

# *Your Heart's Response*

Reflect on a time when you felt far from God but experienced His love and mercy. Write it down and thank Him for finding and restoring you.

_____

_____

_____

_____

_____

_____

_____

_____

_____

_____

_____

_____

_____

_____

_____

_____

_____

_____

_____

_____

_____

## Ponder with Jesus

1. When have you felt most lost, and how did God bring you back to Him?

_____

_____

_____

_____

_____

_____

2. How does knowing Jesus bore the cost of your sins and cast them as far as the east is from the west change the way you see yourself?

_____

_____

_____

_____

_____

3. What specific moment in your life can you reflect on today to remind you of God's forgiveness and unconditional love?

_____

_____

_____

_____

_____

_____

# The Body

The body—each member uniquely crafted,
Designed with purpose, moving as You intended.
A living display of Your love in action.

You move toward people.
You invite the outcast in.
You take the most unlikely, the most different,
And weave them together for Your glory.

Only You could create such unity.
Left to ourselves, we'd give up.
We'd retreat when it gets hard—
Because iron sharpening iron is painful.
Because true community is messy and costly.
But You make it beautiful.

Only You can take strong, unique, imperfect people
And bring them into harmony.
Only You can bind us together,
Not by preference or convenience,
But by the power of Your Spirit,
To walk this world as a reflection of Your kingdom.

It is Your love that sees brokenness and chooses to love anyway.
It is You in us that looks past sin and chooses grace.
If You see Jesus when You look at us,
Then we can also see Jesus in our brothers and sisters.

The world tells us differences divide.
That we should surround ourselves only with those like us.
But in doing so, we would miss the beauty—
The beauty of seeing, even in part,
The fullness of who You are.

## Grace in Focus

This poem is a celebration—a glimpse of the beauty God designed for His people. The Church is not a building; it is a body. A family. A gathering of broken, redeemed, wildly different people—brought together not by sameness, but by Christ Himself. We are not called to be alike. We are called to be one. "Just as a body, though one, has many parts, but all its many parts form one body, so it is with Christ." (1 Corinthians 12:12 NIV) Each of us were created uniquely—with different gifts, different personalities, different roles. The world tells us to fear those differences, to build walls instead of bridges. But Jesus whispers something different. "I have made you for each other." "See what I see." "Love as I have loved you." Just as God chose to see us through the lens of Jesus' sacrifice, we are called to see others through the same grace-filled lens. The Church, though messy and imperfect, is His chosen vessel—a living, breathing testament of His love. We don't have to look the same, think the same, or move the same to be part of His Kingdom. Our unity isn't found in agreement—it's found in Christ alone. So today, listen for His whisper. Step toward the ones who are different. Love boldly. Build bridges. See with His eyes. This is the beauty of His Church. This is the power of the gospel.

## A Moment with God

Lord, thank You for creating me as a unique part of Your body. Help me to value the differences in others and to see them through Your eyes. Teach me to love with Your grace and to work in unity with others to bring Your kingdom to earth. In Jesus' name, Amen.

# Your Heart's Response

Think about someone in your life who is different from you but part of God's family. How can you celebrate their uniqueness and work together to point people to Jesus this week?

_____

_____

_____

_____

_____

_____

_____

_____

_____

_____

_____

_____

_____

_____

_____

_____

_____

_____

_____

_____

_____

*Ponder with Jesus*

1. How does knowing you are a unique part of God's body encourage you today?

_____

_____

_____

_____

_____

_____

2. What is one way you can embrace someone's differences to reflect God's love?

_____

_____

_____

_____

_____

_____

3. How can you contribute to unity within the body of Christ?

_____

_____

_____

_____

_____

_____

# No Matter

Lord, let my heart long for You—
Not just for what You give.
Why do I desire who You make me
More than I desire You?

I'm sorry, Lord.
I love the way You shape me,
But sometimes, I love that more than I love You.
Change my heart. Forgive me.
Awaken a longing for You above all else.

Not my performance,
Not the impact I make,
Not the words I say—
Let my satisfaction be in You alone.
Let me rest in who You are,
Not in what I can do.

Even when I wrestle,
Even when I pull away,
Even when I can't stand myself—
Your love remains.
No conditions. No ifs. No strings attached.
Not a call to behavior modification,
But a heart transformed by grace.

So, Father, change me.
Shape my heart to love You most.
And I will trust—
You will finish the good work You began in me.

## Grace in Focus

This poem beautifully captures the heartbeat of the gospel: God's love is not something we strive for—it's something we live from. We don't have to earn His affection or prove our worth. His love is steady, unshaken, and unconditional (Ephesians 1:5-6 NIV). It is not based on how well we perform, how strong our faith feels, or how much we serve—it is rooted in who He is. Jesus' death and resurrection sealed our identity in the Father's heart forever. No mistake can undo it. No striving can make Him love us more. We are already fully His. And in the quiet, He whispers to us: "You are already loved. Stop hiding in shame—just come." "You don't have to do more to be mine. You already are." "Be still and know that I am God." When we let this truth sink in, we step into who we were always meant to be. No longer chasing worth, no longer doing to prove—but simply being His. And from that place of being, we begin to live differently. We love freely because we are loved. We serve joyfully because we are secure. We walk boldly because we are His. So today, lean in. Let His love settle deep. Let go of shame. Live from who you already are—His beloved.

## A Moment with God

Lord, thank You for loving me without conditions. Thank You for the gospel, which reminds me that Your love doesn't depend on my performance. Transform my heart so that I long for You above everything else. Help me rest in Your grace and live from a place of freedom and joy. In Jesus' name, Amen.

# Your Heart's Response

Reflect on any ways you've tried to earn God's love through performance. Spend time thanking Him for loving you as you are, and ask Him to deepen your identity in Him.

_____

_____

_____

_____

_____

_____

_____

_____

_____

_____

_____

_____

_____

_____

_____

_____

_____

_____

_____

_____

_____

_____

_____

*Ponder with Jesus*

1. Why do we try to earn God's love?

_____

_____

_____

_____

_____

_____

_____

2. How does knowing His love is unconditional change you?

_____

_____

_____

_____

_____

_____

3. What does it look like for you to accept God's grace?

_____

_____

_____

_____

_____

_____

# *Broken but Held*

I can't catch my breath—
My lungs are full, but not with air.
Every step feels heavier,
Like six more bricks pressing down.

I've never felt this anxious,
Never been this overwhelmed.
My hands are numb, my stomach turns—
I'm drowning in the weight of it all.
My mind shouts, *You can't do this*.
The pressure builds, wound so tight I might break.

But I am not alone.
I have a Helper—
The One who gives rest to the weary,
Who is strong when I am weak,
Who breathes life into what feels dead.

On Him, I will rest.
Through His strength, I can stand.
For He is the Almighty—
The beginning, the end, and everything I need.

## Grace in Focus

This poem speaks to the moments when life feels too heavy to bear. When anxiety suffocates, when fear creeps in, when the weight of it all feels like it might pull us under. But the gospel reminds us of something greater: we are not alone. Jesus is near. He is not a distant observer but the One who steps into the storm with us. He holds us when we tremble, strengthens us when we falter, and speaks peace into the chaos. And in the middle of it all, He whispers: "I am with you, even here." "You don't have to be strong—I will hold you up." "Be still. I am your peace." Through His sacrifice on the cross, Jesus carried every burden—our sin, our sorrow, our fear—and in exchange, He offers us **rest, strength, and a peace that surpasses understanding** (Philippians 4:7 NIV). We may feel like we're drowning, but His hands are underneath us. We may feel weak, but His strength is made perfect in our weakness. So today, exhale. Let go of the weight. Let His whisper quiet the storm in your soul. He is here. He is faithful. And He will carry you through.

## A Moment with God

Lord, I feel overwhelmed and broken at times, but I know You are my strength. Thank You for the gospel, which assures me that I don't have to carry my burdens alone. Help me rest in Your power and trust that You hold me even when I feel like I'm falling apart. In Jesus' name, Amen.

# Your Heart's Response

Identify one area of your life where you feel overwhelmed. Write it down and pray, asking God to remind you of His strength and presence in that situation.

_____

_____

_____

_____

_____

_____

_____

_____

_____

_____

_____

_____

_____

_____

_____

_____

_____

_____

_____

_____

_____

_____

# Ponder with Jesus

1. When have you felt completely overwhelmed or broken, and how did God meet you in those moments?

_____

_____

_____

_____

_____

_____

2. How does God's promise to never leave you impact your day to day life?

_____

_____

_____

_____

_____

_____

3. What is one practical way you can lean on God's strength this week?

_____

_____

_____

_____

_____

_____

# Grace Covers All

Oh, Your grace

Is given freely to the undeserved,

Is given from a cost so great.

If we had to earn it, we would break.

Oh God, thank You for Your righteousness.


Oh, what a trade I couldn't make—

My sin for Your holy robes,

My treachery for right standing,

My exile for adoption.

Oh God, thank You for Your blood.

## Grace in Focus

The gospel is the greatest exchange—our sin for His righteousness, our shame for His mercy, our brokenness for His wholeness. It's not something we could ever earn, yet Jesus freely gave it, pouring out His love on the cross. Because of this, we don't stand before God as strangers or outcasts—we stand as His beloved children. Fully forgiven. Deeply known. Eternally loved. And even now, in the places where doubt creeps in, Jesus whispers: "You are mine." "Nothing can separate you from My love." (Romans 8:38-39 NIV) "You are fully covered—there is no condemnation here." (Romans 8:1 NIV) Through His sacrifice, we are no longer defined by our past, our failures, or our shame. We are adopted into His family as Heirs to the throne, redeemed, and held by a grace that knows no end. There is no greater love than this.

## A Moment with God

Lord, thank You for the incredible gift of Your righteousness. Thank You for trading Your holiness for my brokenness and for adopting me into Your family. Help me live in the freedom and joy of knowing I am fully covered by Your grace. In Jesus' name, Amen.

# Your Heart's Response

Write down three things God has blessed you with that you didn't earn?
Take a moment to thank Him for His kindness and reflect on how His
relentless love transforms your daily life.

_____

_____

_____

_____

_____

_____

_____

_____

_____

_____

_____

_____

_____

_____

_____

_____

_____

_____

_____

_____

_____

_____

# Ponder with Jesus

1. How does knowing God doesn't even see your sin anymore when He looks at you change the way you view yourself?

_____

_____

_____

_____

_____

_____

2. What is one area of your life where you can rely on God rather than your own efforts?

_____

_____

_____

_____

_____

_____

3. How can you share this grace with someone else today?

_____

_____

_____

_____

_____

_____

# *Longing for Home*

Since childhood, I've carried this unshakable feeling—
A longing for something more,
Like a thirst I couldn't quench,

I never understood it—

Why I felt homesick in a place filled with love,

Why a quiet ache for more followed me
But now I see—it was a gift.
A whisper, a reminder: *I am not home.*

There is more.
A perfect harmony awaits,
A life with my Savior beyond this world.
He placed this longing deep within me—
A desire for eternity, for Him.

Lord, keep my heart set on what is true:
This world is not my home.

With You, in heaven is where I long to be.

## Grace in Focus

This poem speaks to a longing we all feel—that ache deep within, reminding us that this world is not our home. No amount of success, love, or comfort can fully satisfy, because we were made for something more. The gospel tells us why: God has set eternity in our hearts (Ecclesiastes 3:11 NIV). That homesick feeling isn't emptiness—it's a gift. It's a whisper from Jesus, gently reminding us of home. "I have prepared a place for you." (John 14:2 NIV) "You are made for more than this world can offer." "Hold on—I am coming soon." Jesus' life, death, and resurrection paved the way for us to be with Him forever. He took on our sin so nothing could separate us from the Father. And until the day we see Him face to face, our longing keeps us looking toward heaven—our true home. So if you feel restless, if you ache for something this world can't give, lean into the whisper. Let your longing draw you closer to the One who is preparing a place just for you.

## A Moment with God

Lord, thank You for the reminder that this world is not my home. Thank You for the gospel, which assures me that I have a place with You in heaven. Help me to live today with eternity in mind, finding joy and hope in Your promise. In Jesus' name, Amen.

# Your Heart's Response

Take a moment to think about what heaven will be like. Try to even imagine a place with no more sorrow or pain. Ask God to help you to be reminded of heaven and the eternal values this week.

_____

_____

_____

_____

_____

_____

_____

_____

_____

_____

_____

_____

_____

_____

_____

_____

_____

_____

_____

_____

# *Ponder with Jesus*

1. When have you felt the longing for something more?

_____

_____

_____

_____

_____

_____

2. How does the promise of heaven give you hope in your daily life?

_____

_____

_____

_____

_____

_____

3. What is one way you can live today with eternity in mind?

_____

_____

_____

_____

_____

_____

# The Voice that Speaks Life

You've given each of us a voice—
Unique, intentional, unlike anyone else's.
No two sound the same.
You crafted every voice with purpose:
To speak the truth of Jesus, to carry Your
love wherever we go.

If only we truly believed that,
If we knew deep in our bones that our voice
was designed by You—
Oh, how the enemy would tremble.
Because a child of God who knows their
purpose and uses their voice
Can turn this world upside down
With love that sacrifices,
Love that gives without condition.

The enemy's only hope is to silence us.
To make us believe our voice doesn't matter.
That no one cares. That we sound foolish.
The same tired lies he's whispered for gener-
ations—
Hoping we'll stay quiet. Because if he can
keep us silent,
He can try to stop the love of
Jesus from moving through
us,
From breathing life into
others,

From helping people feel truly seen, known,
and loved.

If he keeps us quiet,
He keeps us from being the voice God uses
To awaken dry bones,
To stir hearts with the relentless love of
Jesus—
A love that died for them, that longs to
restore their relationship with the Father
Through His blood and forgiveness.

But imagine the power if God's people
found their voice—
And chose to use it.
To speak boldly, to love fiercely—
Not just those who love us back, but those
who curse us too.
To serve with humility, to fight for love with
both our words and actions.

That's why love must be at the center of it all.
Without love, our words are a hideous noise.
Our actions lose meaning.
But when done in love,
We care for the whole person—body, mind,
and soul.
We serve because we see their worth.
Because they are precious to God.

Because they are the ones Jesus died
for.
And if I use my voice for anything,
Let it be this—
To tell the world about the only One
who gives life,
Who gives purpose, who satisfies
every longing of my heart—
Jesus Christ.

## Grace in Focus

God has placed a voice inside you—a voice that carries His love, His truth, and His purpose. But so often, the enemy tries to silence it. He screams lies: "You have nothing to say." "Your voice doesn't matter." But the gospel speaks the truth. Your worth is not found in how eloquent you are, how bold you feel, or how others respond. Your voice matters because it was given to you by God himself. Jesus used His voice to bring life, to speak truth, to glorify the Father—and now, He invites you to do the same. And when fear tries to steal your words, Jesus whispers: "I have called you to speak." (Jeremiah 1:9 NIV) "My Spirit will give you the words." (Luke 12:12 NIV) "Your voice carries My love." (Colossians 3:16 NIV) When we speak His truth, we bring light into darkness, hope into despair, and healing into broken places. We don't have to be perfect—we just have to be willing.

So today, let His whispers drown out the lies. Speak boldly. Speak truthfully. Speak for His glory. Because your voice was made to echo His.

## A Moment with God

Lord, thank You for the unique voice You've given me. Help me to use it to boldly to share Your love and truth with those around me. Silence the lies of the enemy and remind me that my voice matters because it carries Your message. I pray the Holy Spirit teaches me in that hour what I ought to say (Luke 12:12 NIV). In Jesus' name, Amen.

# Your Heart's Response

Think of one way you can use your voice today to encourage someone or point them to Jesus. Take that step, trusting God to work through you.

_____

_____

_____

_____

_____

_____

_____

_____

_____

_____

_____

_____

_____

_____

_____

_____

_____

_____

_____

_____

# Ponder with Jesus

1. What lies have you believed about the value of your voice?

_____

_____

_____

_____

_____

_____

2. How can the truth of the gospel inspire confidence to speak boldly?

_____

_____

_____

_____

_____

_____

3. Who can you encourage or share God's love with today using your voice?

_____

_____

_____

_____

_____

_____

# Grace that Transforms

How could you love this imperfection?
How could you fix this mess I've made?
Why would you choose my imperfection?
How could you love this ungrateful heart?

You reach out your hand—I turn away.
You offer me life—my flesh chooses death.
You show me what's right—I love evil.
You give me beauty—I pick destruction.

Yet still, You wait.
Still, You open my eyes.
Still, You gave Your Son—for me.

There is no explanation.
This is craziness to me.
You must not be of this world.
You must be something greater,
Something holier than holy,
Something greater than great,
Someone before there was a start.

You are truly our God to be praised.

## Grace in Focus

This poem echoes the profound grace of God—a grace that meets us not at our best, but at our worst. The gospel tells us that while we were still sinners, Christ died for us (Romans 5:8 NIV). Not because we were worthy. Not because we had something to offer. But because His love refused to leave us where we were. Jesus saw our mess and still chose the cross. He stepped into our brokenness, carried our shame, and exchanged it for His right standing with God the Father. His grace doesn't wait for us to have it all together—it comes right where we are and makes us new. And in the moments when we feel unworthy, when we struggle to believe we are loved, He whispers: "I have already chosen you." "You are covered by My grace." "You are not too far gone—I have made you whole." This is the heart of the gospel—a relentless, pursuing love that refuses to let go. A grace that transforms our imperfection into righteousness, our failures into redemption, and our brokenness into beauty. So today, lean in. Let His whispers drown out your doubt. Let grace wash over you. You are His—and that changes everything.

## A Moment with God

Lord, thank You for loving me even when I turn away. Thank You for the gospel, which reminds me that Your grace isn't earned but freely given. Transform my heart and make me more like You. In Jesus' name, Amen.

## Your Heart's Response

Write down one area of your life where you feel unworthy of God's grace. Reflect on how His love has already covered it and thank Him for His transforming power.

_____

_____

_____

_____

_____

_____

_____

_____

_____

_____

_____

_____

_____

_____

_____

_____

_____

_____

_____

_____

_____

_____

# Ponder with Jesus

1. What is one way you've experienced God's grace despite your
   imperfections?

_____

_____

_____

_____

_____

_____

2. How does knowing that God's love is not based on your performance
   bring you peace?

_____

_____

_____

_____

_____

_____

3. What is one step you can take to embrace His grace more fully today?

_____

_____

_____

_____

_____

_____

# Trusting His Timing

Why do I rush ahead?
Why do I question Your plans?
I think I know best,
But my impatience only brings pain.

You work in ways beyond my sight,
Your timing is perfect and good.
Though I may not understand,
You've never failed me yet.

Teach me to wait, Lord,
To trust in Your hands,
To believe that Your plans
Are far greater than my own.

## Grace in Focus

Waiting is hard. We want answers now, solutions quickly, and a timeline we can control. When life feels uncertain, it's easy to wonder if God sees us, if He's really working, if His timing is truly good. But the gospel reminds us of something deeper—God's faithfulness is never on pause. Jesus Himself waited—on the Father's timing, on the fulfillment of promises, even as He faced the cross. And in the waiting, He trusted. Even when God's plans don't match our expectations, His ways are higher. His timing is perfect. His heart is for us. And in the tension of the unknown, He whispers: "I see you." (Genesis 16:13 NIV) "I am working, even now." (Romans 8:28 NIV) "My plans for you are good." (Jeremiah 29:11 NIV) Waiting isn't wasted when it draws us closer to the One who holds the future. It's in the waiting that our faith is refined, our trust deepened, and our hearts aligned with His. So today, lean in. Rest in the whisper. Trust in His timing. He is always faithful.

## A Moment with God

Lord, I confess my impatience and my desire to rush ahead. Thank You for the gospel, which reminds me of Your faithfulness and perfect timing. Help me trust You fully, even when I don't see the whole picture. In Jesus' name, Amen.

## Your Heart's Response

Think about an area in your life where you're struggling to wait on God's timing. Pray for patience and faith, asking Him to help you trust in His plan.

_____

_____

_____

_____

_____

_____

_____

_____

_____

_____

_____

_____

_____

_____

_____

_____

_____

_____

_____

_____

_____

_____

_____

# Ponder with Jesus

1. When and why is waiting on God's timing hard for you?

_____

_____

_____

_____

_____

_____

2. How does remembering God's faithfulness in the past help you trust
   Him today?

_____

_____

_____

_____

_____

_____

3. What is one way you can find joy in trusting God's timing?

_____

_____

_____

_____

_____

_____

# Freedom Through Forgiveness

I feel sick—

Why is the Church so divided?

Why do things not turn out?


Don't we have Your Spirit in us?

Why can't we make it work?

So much falls apart.


I do not understand.

Should I have done something?

Is it the enemy?

Or is it You?


Show us what's meant to be.

Make things right.

Make things new.

I don't know what to do.


I throw my flag up.

I can't do anything.

It's in Your hands—

Where everything belongs.

## Grace in Focus

Division is everywhere—in our churches, our families, even within our own hearts. The weight of broken relationships can feel unbearable, the wounds too deep, the distance too wide. But the gospel tells a different story. Jesus came to heal the greatest divide—the one between us and God. His sacrifice on the cross was the bridge, restoring what was lost and making a way for true reconciliation. And if He could do that, is anything really too broken for Him to restore (Ephesians 4:32 NIV)? Even when forgiveness feels impossible, even when unity seems out of reach, He whispers: "I have already made the way." "Let go—I will carry this for you." "My Spirit is working, even when you can't see it." Forgiveness isn't forgetting. Reconciliation isn't instant. But when we surrender our hurts to Him, He begins to heal what we cannot. He softens hardened hearts, mends what's been torn apart, and brings peace where there was once only pain. So today, listen for His whisper. Trust that He is working in the unseen. Release what you've been holding onto. He is the God who restores.

## A Moment with God

Lord, I don't always understand why things fall apart, but I trust You to make things new. Thank You for the gospel, which shows me the power of forgiveness and reconciliation. Help me to release control and trust in Your plan. In Jesus' name, Amen.

# *Your Heart's Response*

Think of a situation where division or brokenness has caused pain in your life. Surrender it to God in prayer, asking Him to bring healing and unity.

_____

_____

_____

_____

_____

_____

_____

_____

_____

_____

_____

_____

_____

_____

_____

_____

_____

_____

_____

_____

_____

*Ponder with Jesus*

1. When have you experienced division that felt impossible to overcome?

_____

_____

_____

_____

_____

_____

2. How does the gospel give you hope even in that situation?

_____

_____

_____

_____

_____

_____

3. What is one step you can take today to pursue peace and forgiveness?

_____

_____

_____

_____

_____

_____

# Strength in Surrender

Lord, I'm afraid.
Anxiety grips my heart,
my chest tightens, my stomach churns.

I fear wasting time,
choosing wrong,
doing too much, yet never enough.
I question my purpose,
wonder if I measure up,
feel the weight of needing to get it right.

When I fall short, I hide—
from You, from others, from grace itself.
Why do I believe I must be perfect?
This prison of pressure keeps me
from seeing the goodness around me,
from resting in what You've already done.

I'm weary, Lord.
I need Your peace,
Your holiness,
Your rest.

I am not God.
I will never be perfect.
Let me rest in Your perfection.

## Grace in Focus

Anxiety and perfectionism shout the same exhausting lie: "You're not enough." So we push harder, strive more, trying to meet impossible standards—trying to prove that we are valuable. But no matter how much we do, it never feels like enough. But Jesus speaks a better word. The gospel reminds us that He has already met every standard, fulfilled every requirement, and done what we never could (Romans 8:3-4 NIV). His life, death, and resurrection set us free from hustling—free from the need to earn our worth or prove our value. And in the moments when we feel like we're falling short, He whispers: "You don't have to do more—I have already done it all." "You are not defined by what you achieve but by your place as My child." True strength isn't found in doing more—it's found in surrender. In laying down the pressure, the fear, the need to be perfect, and simply resting in Jesus' power and goodness. So today, exhale. Let go of striving. Lean into His whisper. His grace is sufficient—His love is enough. And because you are His, so are you.

## A Moment with God

Lord, I surrender my fears and anxieties to You. Thank You for the gospel, which reminds me that I don't have to strive for perfection because Jesus was perfect on my behalf. Help me to rest in Your grace and trust in Your sufficiency. In Jesus' name, Amen.

# Your Heart's Response

Take a moment to identify an area where you're striving to be perfect. Write it down and pray, asking God to remind you of His grace and to help you let go of the need to strive and hide in shame.

_____

_____

_____

_____

_____

_____

_____

_____

_____

_____

_____

_____

_____

_____

_____

_____

_____

_____

_____

_____

# Ponder with Jesus

1. What fears or anxieties are you holding onto that keep you from experiencing God's peace?

_____

_____

_____

_____

_____

_____

2. How does the gospel remind you that you don't have to be perfect?

_____

_____

_____

_____

_____

_____

3. What is one way you can show compassion to yourself today?

_____

_____

_____

_____

_____

_____

# His Hands Hold Me

When I placed my heart
Before Your gracious, welcoming heart,
You gently held it in Your hands—
So much care and love-filled hands.

I should have turned to You sooner;
The relief I would have felt,
The difference now and then
Is life-giving.

Your power is majestic.
Your beauty is worthy of praise.

## Grace in Focus

The hands of God—tender yet strong, gentle yet mighty. The same hands that shaped the heavens are the hands that hold you now. The gospel reminds us that Jesus stretched out His hands on the cross—not just to save us, but to carry us, hold us, and never let us go. His hands are the place where we find security when we feel unsteady, healing when we feel broken, and strength when we are weak. And in the moments when we feel lost, forgotten, or too far gone, He whispers: "I have written your name on the palms of My hands." (Isaiah 49:16 NIV) "I will never leave you." "I am holding you—even now." His hands are not distant. They are near, always reaching, always ready to lift us up. Through every trial, every storm, every moment of doubt, we are never alone. So today, lean into His whisper. Rest in the hands that were pierced for you. You are held, you are seen, and you are deeply loved.

## A Moment with God

Lord, thank You for holding my heart with such love and care. Thank You for the gospel, which assures me that I am secure in Your hands. Teach me to trust You fully and to rest in Your constant presence. In Jesus' name, Amen.

# Your Heart's Response

Spend a moment today reflecting on how God has held you through difficult times. Write down a specific example and thank Him for His faithfulness.

_____

_____

_____

_____

_____

_____

_____

_____

_____

_____

_____

_____

_____

_____

_____

_____

_____

_____

_____

_____

_____

_____

_____

# Ponder with Jesus

1. When have you felt the comfort of being held by God?

_____

_____

_____

_____

_____

_____

2. How does Jesus' sacrifice on the cross remind you of His care for you?

_____

_____

_____

_____

_____

_____

3. What is one way you can trust God to carry you through a current challenge?

_____

_____

_____

_____

_____

_____

# Strength in the Unknown

For the first time in a long time,
I don't even know what I feel.

It's like I feel everything...
and nothing...
all at once.

Lies swirl in my mind,
and my spirit wrestles—
fighting to take them captive.

But sometimes...
sometimes the enemy wins.
And I slip back into old patterns,
old ways I thought were gone.

And oh, how I hate it.
How I hate the version of me
without Jesus.

I need Him—desperately—
to cleanse my heart once more,
to make me whole again.

Without Him, I'm just a broken puzzle
piece—
lost, out of place,
with nowhere to belong.

But with Him...
He takes even the broken pieces
and places them perfectly
into His masterpiece—
this mission, this life
woven with purpose and grace.

So, Lord...
Soften my heart.
Break through the walls I don't even
know how to tear down.
I don't know where to begin—
but I know You do.

I'm sorry, God.
I've sinned against You.
And I can't—
I won't—do this life without You.
I need all of You.

Humble me again,
draw me closer,
because I know You can...
and I know You will.

## Grace in Focus

When we feel lost, unsure, or like life is just a mess of broken pieces, the gospel holds us steady. Even when we can't see the way forward, Jesus is already there—guiding, restoring, weaving our lives into something greater than we can imagine. It's easy to believe that our brokenness disqualifies us, that our shortcomings or doubts mean we're failing. But God doesn't waste anything. The very places where we feel most lost are often where He is doing His greatest work. What feels uncertain to us is already known to Him. And in the moments when fear creeps in, when the unknown feels overwhelming, He whispers: "I am with you, even here." (Isaiah 41:10 NIV) "I know the way—just follow Me." "What feels broken, I am making new." Trusting Him when we can't see the outcome is an act of faith, a surrender to the One who never lets go. His hands are shaping our lives, fitting every piece into His masterpiece, turning what was meant for our harm into something beautiful (Genesis 50:20 NIV). So today, lean in. Let go of the need to see the whole picture. Trust the whisper of the One who does. He is leading you, He is working for your good, and He is always, always faithful.

## A Moment with God

Lord, in my confusion and uncertainty, remind me of Your steadfast love. Thank You for the gospel, which assures me that You are my guide and my hope. Use me as part of Your beautiful plan, and help me trust You fully. In Jesus' name, Amen.

# Your Heart's Response

Spend time reflecting on an area where you feel uncertain. Pray for God's guidance and write down a verse that reminds you that He is trustworthy.

_____

_____

_____

_____

_____

_____

_____

_____

_____

_____

_____

_____

_____

_____

_____

_____

_____

_____

_____

_____

_____

# Ponder with Jesus

1. When have you felt most confused about your purpose, and how did God meet you in that moment?

_____

_____

_____

_____

_____

_____

2. How does trusting in God's bigger plan give you peace?

_____

_____

_____

_____

_____

_____

3. What is one way you can step forward in faith, even when the path feels unclear?

_____

_____

_____

_____

_____

_____

# Seeing Clearly

Thank You for opening my eyes—
for showing me who You are and who I am in You.
I cannot do this alone.
I need Your goodness to cover me,
to cleanse me, to redeem and renew me.

Even my best efforts fall short—
tainted with pride, tangled in striving.
I do what I don't want to do,
and what I long to do, I fail to do.
I cannot save myself.
Every place I've turned has promised life,
yet only left me empty, longing for more.

I need a Savior.
I need a Rescuer.
I need a Redeemer.
Without You, I am lost.
But in You—I am chosen.
I am Your daughter.
I am whole.
I am royalty.
I am perfectly loved.

## Grace in Focus

This poem is raw, real, and honest—a confession we all carry deep within. We need Jesus. No matter how hard we try, how much we strive, how well we perform, we will always fall short of perfection (Romans 3:23 NIV). But grace meets us there. The gospel isn't about trying harder; it's about surrendering to the One who has already done it all. Through Jesus, we are redeemed, washed clean, and made completely new. Our identity is no longer lost, broken, or unworthy—instead, we are chosen, beloved, and whole in Him. And when shame weighs heavy and exhaustion takes hold, Jesus leans in and whispers: "I have called you by name—you are Mine." (Isaiah 43:1 NIV) "Come as you are—I will make you new." "You are fully known, fully loved, and fully held." This is the beauty of God's love—it takes us exactly as we are and transforms us into something entirely new. So today, rest in His whisper. Let grace do what only grace can. You are already His.

## A Moment with God

Lord, thank You for opening my eyes to see my need for You. Thank You for the gospel, which assures me that I am redeemed and loved, not because of what I do, but because of who You are. Help me to live in this freedom and reflect Your love to others. In Jesus' name, Amen.

# Your Heart's Response

Reflect on areas where you've tried to rely on your own strength. Write them down and pray, asking God to remind you that He is enough.

_____

_____

_____

_____

_____

_____

_____

_____

_____

_____

_____

_____

_____

_____

_____

_____

_____

_____

_____

_____

_____

# Ponder with Jesus

1. In what areas is it easy to recognize your need for Jesus and in what areas is it more difficult to recognize?

_____

_____

_____

_____

_____

_____

2. What does it mean to you to be chosen and perfectly loved by God?

_____

_____

_____

_____

_____

_____

3. How does recognizing your need for Jesus change how you approach your struggles?

_____

_____

_____

_____

_____

_____

# Free in Him

Free. Something I thought I was ten years ago.
But each year, God removes
Shackle after shackle.

He started with the biggest of all—
Freedom from sin and death.
I am no longer a slave to myself.
And when I thought I couldn't get any freer,
God reveals my captivity
And delivers me from it.

He really does use what was meant for our harm
For our good.

He uses my grief to show His strength,
To reveal my idols,
To renew my zeal for Him,
And to help me find my voice.

For too long, I was silenced by the enemy,
Believing the lie my voice did not matter.

God showed me my priorities.
He molded me to be gentle and unhurried—
To sit and linger in His beauty: His creation,
His Word, and with His children.

I praise You, Jesus.
In Your freedom, I find who You made me to be.
Here, exactly where I am,
With the scars and skills You've given me.
Ready to give an answer for the irrefutable hope
I carry inside me of Your never-failing love.

## Grace in Focus

Freedom in Christ is so much more than just freedom from sin—it's the freedom to be fully who God created you to be. No more chains. No more shame. No more being defined by your past or your failures. Through the gospel, Jesus breaks every chain, not just to set us free, but to lead us into a life of purpose, fullness, and joy. He steps into our weakness with His strength. He takes our pain and redeems it for His glory (Isaiah 61:1-2 NIV). He renews us, reshapes us, and gives us power to walk boldly in His love. And when we doubt if we're really free, when fear tries to pull us back, Jesus whispers: "You are no longer a slave to sin—you are My child." (Galatians 4:7 NIV) "Your past does not define you—I do." "Step forward, unafraid—I have gone before you." In Him, we are free to speak with boldness, love sacrificially, and live with confidence in the identity He has given us. So today, let His whisper be louder than your fear. Step into the freedom He has already won for you. You are His—and in Him, you are fully free.

## A Moment with God

Lord, thank You for setting me free. Thank You for the gospel, which frees me from sin and gives me new life. Teach me to live in that freedom, to trust Your plans, and to share the hope You've given me with others. In Jesus' name, Amen.

# Your Heart's Response

Write down one area where you still feel bound and share it with a trusted friend. Ask God to reveal His truth over that area, and with a trusted friend, boldly claim the freedom that is yours in Jesus' powerful name.

# Ponder with Jesus

1. What does freedom in Christ look like to you?

_____

_____

_____

_____

_____

_____

2. How has God used your struggles or grief to reveal His strength?

_____

_____

_____

_____

_____

_____

3. What is one way you can walk in freedom today, trusting in His love?

_____

_____

_____

_____

_____

_____

# The Father's Voice

You told me I'm worthless,
But my Father says *I'm worth it.*

You told me I'm only worth what I give,
But my Father says *He just wants me.*

You told me I have to prove my worth,
But my Father says, *"I have already proven your worth."*

You told me I have to earn love,
But my Father says *there's nothing that can take His love from me.*

You told me I'm not worth saving,
But my Father says *I'm worth His only Son's life.*

You told me I have to pay for a good life,
But my Father says, *"Jesus paid it all."*

You told me I'm nothing special,
But my Father says *there's none like me.*

You told me a man's desire holds my value,
But my Father says *I am seated at His right hand.*

You told me no one cares what I say,
But my Father says, *"I gave you your voice."*

You told me to be ashamed of what I've done,
But my Father says, *"Come to Me."*

You told me to hide myself,
But my Father says, *"My blood covers you."*

You told me it'd be better if I were dead,
But my Father says, *"I've made you to live."*

You told me to hate myself,
But my Father says, *"I created you."*

## Grace in Focus

The world is loud. The enemy is relentless. Lie after lie tries to take root in our hearts: "You're not enough." "You're unworthy." "You'll never be truly loved." But the gospel speaks a different story. A story of love, redemption, and undeniable worth. Jesus' life, death, and resurrection declare the truth over us: we are deeply loved, fully forgiven, and eternally valuable. God did not spare His own Son but gave Him up for us (Romans 8:32 NIV), proving once and for all just how much we mean to Him. And in the middle of the noise, when doubt creeps in, Jesus whispers: "You are Mine, and I will never let you go." "I have paid the price—you are worth everything to Me." "My love for you will never change." His voice is the only truth that matters. And when we listen— when we let His words drown out the lies—we find freedom, peace, and assurance that we are His. So today, lean into His whisper. Silence the lies. Stand in truth. You are chosen, loved, and completely secure in Him.

## A Moment with God

Lord, thank You for silencing the lies of the enemy with Your truth. Thank You for the gospel, which assures me that I am deeply loved and eternally valuable to You. Help me to hear Your voice above all others and rest in the truth of who I am in Christ. In Jesus' name, Amen.

# Your Heart's Response

Identify a lie you've been believing about yourself and write it down. Then, replace it with the truth of God's Word. Hold onto that truth throughout the day, refusing to let the lie take root in your mind. Take that lie captive and walk in the freedom Christ has given you.

_____

_____

_____

_____

_____

_____

_____

_____

_____

_____

_____

_____

_____

_____

_____

_____

_____

_____

_____

# Ponder with Jesus

1. What lies about yourself have you believed, and how has God's truth countered them?

_____

_____

_____

_____

_____

_____

2. What does the gospel show you about your worth?

_____

_____

_____

_____

_____

3. What steps can you take to listen to the Father's voice more intentionally this week?

_____

_____

_____

_____

_____

_____

# The Gift of Intimacy

Oh, what a gift true intimacy is.
God made the perfect place for us to
experience it—

A place of safety,
Where you wouldn't fear abandonment,
Where you wouldn't fear conditions,
Where you wouldn't fear abuse or neglect,
Where you wouldn't fear being objectified.

A place called marriage—
An unconditional, eternal, comfy blanket.

Only here is it truly safe
To let down your veil,
And show your truest thoughts,
Your deepest desires,
And your unashamed body.

Only in this environment—
God made for your protection
And absolute pleasure and joy—
Are you united on every level with someone,
Solely based on a covenant,
Independent of their actions.

No matter what, you love
anyway.
You choose unity over
winning,
Drawing closer over

withdrawing,
Finding the beauty in your own marriage
Over fantasizing about another one.

Oh, how I wish I knew that
The lustful desires of a man
Are not the loving intimacy You designed,
God.

How it is only a cheap, cheap imitation
The devil uses to kill, steal, and destroy your
heart.

How it wreaked havoc on my heart,
Believing such powerful lies about
What I thought love looked like.

Now, thank God, I see the truth:
God is love.
Jesus dying for the undeserved is the proof.
And through our spouse, He gives us the gift
To experience even a fraction of such an
intimate relationship.

Physical love is just a part of it—
Letting another person see your heart with
no facades,
Letting them see you at your most
vulnerable,
When you feel the most unattractive,
Letting them see you at your happiest, your

most numb.

They have a front-row seat
Each day to see all of you—
For all that you are.

It's a love that sees them
Through God's eyes—
As the heir to His throne they are.

And it is through that pure love

That you connect sexually,
Putting each other's needs first,
And making a baby out of the love
You have for each other.

Not lusting after an object,
But loving their entire being—
The good and the not-so-pretty.

You choose them—
Again and again.

## Grace in Focus

Marriage isn't just about sharing life with someone—it's a small picture of the way Jesus loves us. He didn't wait for us to have it all together. He loved first, fully, and forever— and He proved it by giving His life for us on the cross (Ephesians 5:21–33 NIV).

That's the kind of love marriage invites us into. Not keeping score. Not loving only when it's easy. But choosing to love even when it costs something. And the truth is, we can't do that on our own. We need God's help every step of the way.

In the moments when patience runs low, when selfishness sneaks in, or when connection feels far away—God is right there. His Spirit gives us the strength to stay, to forgive, to serve, to start fresh. Marriage isn't meant to be perfect—it's meant to point to a perfect love.

So let your marriage be a glimpse of something greater. A reminder that love isn't just a feeling—it's a choice backed by action. Just like Jesus showed us. Let Him hold you together, and let your love story reflect the one that changes everything.

## A Moment with God

Lord, thank You for the gift of intimacy in marriage. Thank You for the gospel, which shows me how to love selflessly and sacrificially. Teach me to reflect Your love in my relationship, to honor the covenant You've given us, and to grow closer to You through it. In Jesus' name, Amen.

# Your Heart's Response

Spend intentional time with the person you're closest to this week, focusing on open communication and mutual encouragement. Take time to share and explore your thoughts on what intimacy truly means.

# Ponder with Jesus

1. What makes you feel truly known and loved in a relationship?

_____

_____

_____

_____

_____

2. Can you think of moments when God has gently pursued your heart—
   when He's reminded you that you're deeply known and loved? If nothing
   comes to mind right now, that's okay. Ask Him to show you. Perfect intimacy
   comes from Him—the One who knows us fully and loves us completely.

_____

_____

_____

_____

_____

3. What is one small way you can choose connection over distance in your
   closest relationship today?

_____

_____

_____

_____

_____

# Focus on What Matters

Distractions... they... they... wait...
what... oh...
Distract you.

Not only do they distract you,
But they pretend they'll fill you.

They offer a quick feel-good,
But it flees almost instantly.

Cheap imitations of the real thing.
If they can just get you to believe it's
real—
And good for you—
It'll keep you running back.

Processed sugar steals away
The rich pleasure of enjoying God's
dessert—fruit.

TV shows make you feel seen,
Like you're part of something...
Until the series ends,
And you realize you spent 80 hours
binge-watching a show
Because your dopamine chased the
spikes.

Meanwhile, you haven't seen a real
person in weeks.

Oh, how loneliness reverberates
with a vengeance.
If only there were another show—
Another storyline—

To fill the longing to numb out,
To pretend to live a different life...
One where it all works out.
There go three more weeks—
Of my life. My time.
Time I can't get back.

I don't even want to think about
what I could
Have done with that time instead...

Three date nights—connecting with
my husband.
Two girls' nights—confiding in each
other.
Three days—playing and making
memories with my boys.
Two run-ins with friends.
Five moments—meeting someone
new.
Four poems... one book.
And 100% more emotionally and
physically healthy.

That's just a slim list of what
Socially acceptable binge-watching
has stolen.

Wake. Scroll. Work—
Either work my butt off, or feel
bored.
Eat dinner. Watch or play videos.
Rest.
Repeat—five to seven times a week.

And then I wonder why life feels
meaningless...
Why anxiety and depression are
constant companions.

I haven't even stepped outside
To enjoy the beauty of nature
With all my senses—
In what feels like forever.

I don't accept this life.
I refuse it.

I reject it.
I will pursue stillness.
I will pursue quiet.
I will give my soul
The things God created it to need:

Nature.
A community of people who know
me—truly know me.
Rest.
Fulfilling work.

## Grace in Focus

Distractions are everywhere, promising joy, escape, or fulfillment, but they always leave us feeling emptier than before. They pull our hearts in a thousand directions, stealing our attention from the One who truly satisfies. The gospel reminds us that nothing in this world will ever be enough—except Christ. Jesus doesn't just offer life—He is life. He calls us to turn our focus away from fleeting pleasures and set our eyes on what truly lasts: His kingdom, His presence, His love (Matthew 6:33 NIV). And when the noise of the world tries to drown Him out, Jesus whispers: "Come to Me—I am what your heart is longing for." "You don't need more—you need Me." "Fix your eyes on what is eternal." When we seek Him first, we don't miss out—we step into fullness. The distractions lose their grip, the striving fades, and we find peace, purpose, and joy that nothing else can give. So today, pause. Listen for His whisper. Fix your eyes on Jesus—and find the life your soul has been searching for all along.

## A Moment with God

Lord, help me to see through the distractions that pull me away from You. Thank You for the gospel, which reminds me that You are my ultimate satisfaction. Teach me to focus on what matters most and to rest in Your presence. In Jesus' name, Amen.

# Your Heart's Response

Identify one distraction in your life and think through what all it is costing you. Commit to limiting or removing it this week, and replace it with something that nourishes your soul and write down the ways it changes your days.

*Ponder with Jesus*

1. What deeper longing or need might this distraction be trying to fill?

_____

_____

_____

_____

_____

_____

2. When do you feel most drawn to this distraction—what emotions or thoughts tend to trigger it?

_____

_____

_____

_____

_____

_____

3. How would your heart and mind feel if you truly rested in God instead of seeking temporary relief?

_____

_____

_____

_____

_____

_____

# New Mercies Every Morning

Oh, how grateful I am that every morning is new.
Every morning You meet us
With the free gift of grace in Your right hand
And mercy in Your left.
Every morning, You're giving us what we don't deserve
And have not earned.

Every morning, we have no lack.
You promise to provide everything we need,
Exactly when we need it.
If we would just acknowledge You,
You will make our path straight.

Every morning, You provide a way out of temptation,
For You have overcome it all.
You do not leave us helpless or defenseless.
Like a good Father, You equip us every morning
With what we need.

All we need to do is ask.
Your Spirit in us is strong and willing,
Even when our flesh is weak.
When we are unfaithful, You remain faithful.

Every morning when evil is meant for our harm,
You have already thought out a redemptive plan—
To use it for our good,
To restore beauty and purpose to the broken.

Every morning, You fill us up with Your love
Until it overflows.
May it seep into every part of my body
As my protective armor.
Nothing can break through Your love.
It protects me, covers me,
And makes me more like You every morning.

## Grace in Focus

Every morning, as the sun rises, God's mercy rises with it. His faithfulness is constant, His grace never runs out (Lamentations 3:22-23 NIV). No matter what yesterday held—failures, regrets, weariness—today is covered in fresh mercy. The gospel reminds us that we don't wake up to condemnation—we wake up to love and a clean slate. Jesus' death and resurrection have already secured our redemption, and each new day is another invitation to walk in His strength, not our own. And in the quiet of the morning, before the weight of the day settles in, Jesus whispers: "My grace is enough for today." "You don't have to carry yesterday—I have already redeemed it." "Walk with Me—I will give you all you need." His love never wavers. His provision never fails. He meets us where we are, fills us with His strength, and draws us closer to His heart. So today, take a deep breath. Let go of yesterday. Step into His new mercies. He is with you, and His grace is more than enough.

## A Moment with God

Lord, thank You for the new mercies You provide every morning. Thank You for the gospel, which equips me to live with hope and purpose. Help me to embrace Your grace each day and walk confidently in Your love. In Jesus' name, Amen.

# Your Heart's Response

Each morning this week, take a moment to thank God for His constant grace and mercy. Ask Him to give you what you need each day and every hour. "Fear the LORD, you his holy people, for those who fear him lack nothing." (Psalm 34:9 NIV) If you make a mistake, don't let it ruin your day—accept His grace, forgive yourself, and keep going. See how it changes your mindset and brings peace.

# Ponder with Jesus

1. How does beginning your day with gratitude shift your heart and mindset?

_____

_____

_____

_____

_____

_____

2. When have you experienced God providing exactly what you needed in a moment of weakness?

_____

_____

_____

_____

_____

_____

3. What simple habit could help you stay aware of His presence throughout your day?

_____

_____

_____

_____

_____

_____

# The Beauty of Humility

A beautiful character trait overlooked in today's world.
A trait viewed as weak, a doormat, soft, reckless.

But it is immensely valuable.
The opposite of it is pride.
And pride puts you at odds with the Almighty God.
But humility... humility is not just a character trait or a thing to be modeled,
But really more of a heart posture.

The more humble we become, the closer we are to God,
Because it pushes out pride,
Which is the chasm between us and God.
And humility chips away at that,
And we get to experience God more and more.

Because we now have a right view of how caring, big, and perfect
Our Father in heaven is.
And how we are His creation.
He is the molder, and we are the clay.
And yet He chooses to seat us on the throne next to King Jesus.

Humility is power under control.
Humility is stepping down from Your throne in heaven,
Becoming a helpless baby,
Living in this sinful world to live a perfect life,
And eventually dying for the people who sinned against You.

Jesus put us before Himself.

Us, people who would hurt Him,

And beg for a murderer to be released

And for Jesus to be nailed on a tree.

Who recklessly loves us way more than we deserve,

Just because He does.

Because we are His children.

## Grace in Focus

True humility isn't weakness—it's strength surrendered to God. Jesus, the King of Kings, chose humility. He stepped down from His throne, walked among us, and laid down His life in love (Philippians 2:7 NIV). The gospel reminds us that we don't have to chase recognition or strive for approval—we are already seen, already known, already loved. Our identity is secure in Christ. Pride pulls us away from Him, convincing us we must prove ourselves. But humility draws us near, making room for His love, His power, His presence. And in the moments when we feel unseen or unworthy, Jesus whispers: "You don't have to prove yourself—I have already chosen you." "Lay it down—I am enough for you." "Come lower, and you will find more of Me." Humility isn't about thinking less of ourselves—it's about thinking more of Him. It's the posture that allows us to see Him clearly, love others deeply, and reflect His heart to the world. So today, listen to His whisper. Let go of proving. Step into the quiet strength of humility and see how close you feel to God.

## A Moment with God

Lord, thank You for the humility of Jesus, who gave everything to save me. Thank You for the gospel, which reminds me that my worth is secure in You. Help me to put aside pride and adopt a heart of humility, trusting in Your strength and reflecting Your love. In Jesus' name, Amen.

# Your Heart's Response

Sit with God and ask Him to gently reveal any place in your heart where pride is keeping you at a distance from Him. How might surrendering that to Him open you to receive His love more fully? Let His grace soften you, drawing you into deeper dependence and trust. And if you're willing to trust Him deeply, I encourage you to pray, "Humble me, no matter the cost, because being close to You is the best place to be." This prayer has transformed my life and brought a closeness to God I am forever thankful for.

# Ponder with Jesus

1. What does Jesus' entire life—His birth in a manger, His servant heart, His death on a cross—teach us about the power of humility?

_____

_____

_____

_____

_____

_____

2. What does humility look like in your life?

_____

_____

_____

_____

_____

_____

3. How can embracing humility help you grow closer to Christ and others?

_____

_____

_____

_____

_____

_____

# Love that Reflects Christ

The world will tell you to be loved
Is to never stop feeling the blissful butterflies
kind of love—
A romantic love, a love that makes you
happy all the time.
And if that stops, it's run its course, and
they're not the one.

90s Disney princess movies repeat the story:
The girl waits her whole life to meet the
man.
And it's love at first sight.
He rescues her, whisks her off into the
sunset.
No problems to be had. They were soulmates
forever.

But what if there is more to marriage than
romance and feelings?
What if that is only one portion of its
beauty?

The longer I'm married, the more I find out
other aspects of love,
And see what different kinds of love look
like.
Love from your spouse isn't just candles,
dancing, and sweet talking.

Love is getting married and
giving me years to figure out
how to truly be a wife.
It's being patient enough not to
control me, but giving the Spirit room to do
His work and shape my heart.
Love is, even after the first few years of
getting so many things wrong, still choosing
me as his other half.
Love is noticing—more and more—what I
do for him, and him eager to reciprocate.

Love is praying over me when I'm pregnant
and nauseous,
Asking God to give him the symptoms
instead.
Love is comforting me as I'm pushing out
our sons.
Love is changing as many diapers as he can
to help.

Love is taking out the trash when it's
forgotten.
Love is biting my tongue to speak life
instead of venom.
Love is putting my spouse before my kids,
Choosing unity over winning.

Love is seeing their outright sin and
choosing them anyway.
Love is being one, pushing through the
uncomfortableness of intimacy,
And speaking words of admiration and
gratitude
That connect your hearts over and over
again.

If you see love only through a romantic lens,
You're missing the most fulfilling and soul-
quaking type of relationship here on earth.
Marriage is the closest representation of
Christ's love for His Church,
The love that lays down its life for the other.

Two becoming one is beautiful, grueling,
and counterintuitive,
But Jesus meets you there with open arms
and wisdom.

## Grace in Focus

The world will tell you that love should always feel effortless—that if you have to work at it, something must be wrong. That love should always be thrilling, romantic, and full of excitement, and if it's not, you must have married the wrong person. But the gospel tells a different story. Marriage is not built on fleeting emotions but on a covenant—a promise that mirrors Christ's love for us (Ephesians 5:25 NIV). Jesus didn't love us because we were perfect or easy to love. He saw our failures, our selfishness, our brokenness, and chose us anyway. That's the kind of love marriage calls us to. Not just a love that feels good, but a love that stays. A love that fights for unity when it would be easier to walk away. A love that forgives when every part of you wants to hold on to the hurt. A love that reflects the relentless grace of God. And in this, even our spouse's weaknesses become a gift. Because when we expect them to meet every need, we will always be disappointed. But when we let those disappointments remind us that only Jesus can fully satisfy us, our hearts are set free. Instead of placing impossible expectations on another person, we get to receive their love as a beautiful, imperfect reflection of Christ's perfect love. And in those moments—when love feels hard, when forgiveness feels impossible—Jesus whispers: "Love as I have loved you." "Lay down your pride—grace is stronger." "I am holding your marriage in My hands." Marriage was never meant to be a fairy tale. It was meant to transform us, to shape us, to draw us deeper into the heart of God. When we lean into Him, we find the strength to love boldly, to serve humbly, and to reflect the gospel in the way we love one another.

## A Moment with God

Lord, thank You for the gift of marriage and the way it reflects Your love for us. Thank You for the gospel, which teaches me how to love sacrificially and uncon-ditionally. Help me to honor my spouse, choose love every day, and reflect Your grace in my marriage. In Jesus' name, Amen.

# Your Heart's Response

Think of one way you can selflessly love your spouse or the person you're closest to this week. Whether it's through words of encouragement, an act of service, or simply being present, let your actions reflect the love of Jesus that truly sees people.

*Ponder with Jesus*

1. How does understanding Christ's love for the Church change your view of marriage?

_____

_____

_____

_____

_____

_____

2. What fears or expectations hold you back from fully embracing sacrificial love?

_____

_____

_____

_____

_____

_____

3. How can you live in light of the beautiful picture of the gospel?

_____

_____

_____

_____

_____

_____

# The Gift of Grief

Grief,
It does something to you.
It changes who you are.
From God, you seem really far,
But it really just lowers the bar.

All the stuff that used to matter
Just doesn't anymore.

The world keeps moving.
It doesn't wait or grieve for no one.

I don't know what hurts more—
That it doesn't wait
Or that it feels like you never were.

I can't imagine twenty more years
Without you near.
It seems like a distant memory.

Stupid stuff fades away.
The only thing that matters is following God.
Everything else ends.
Everything else is in vain.

But giving every second of your life to God stays.
It remains eternal.
As an old person sits and watches their family in a rocking chair,
I can't wait to watch from heaven
God water the seeds I gave my life to grow.

Now that has purpose.
To that, I can crawl through life with bloody knees.
I can proudly wear every wrinkle and bruise.
For when I enter Your courts, I want to say I gave it all—
Not a striving "all" that is me having something to prove,
But a reckless, risky life of love lived.

God, I hate grief,
But I love everything good it's done to me.
Like a shock to the spirit,
I am dead to distractions
And awakened to the beautiful, surrendered, free enjoyment
Of the simple, obedient, and abundant life You offer.

Thank You for never leaving me.
Thank You for sparing me.
Thank You for Your mercy.
You are a God of miracles.
You are in every single detail.

You gave me the strength to fight,
The strength to wait in the unknown,
And now the strength to rest.

To El Roi, our God who sees and seeks recompense.

## Grace in Focus

Grief has a way of revealing what truly matters. It strips away distractions, shatters illusions, and brings us to the feet of Jesus. In the ache of loss, we are reminded that everything in this world fades—except what is eternal. And this is where the gospel meets us. Jesus didn't stay distant from our suffering—He stepped into it. He carried our sorrows, bore our pain, and overcame death itself (Isaiah 53:4 NIV). His resurrection declares that loss is not the end, and every tear, every broken heart, every ache in our soul is seen by the Father. And when the weight of grief feels unbearable, when the questions are louder than the answers, Jesus whispers: "I see you." "I am near the brokenhearted." (Psalm 34:18 NIV) "Because I live, you also will live." (John 14:19 NIV) Grief doesn't destroy us—it awakens us. It reminds us that we were made for more than this life, that our purpose isn't just to endure but to live with eternity in mind. So today, let His whisper steady your heart. Lay your sorrow at His feet, trust Him with what you cannot see, and keep sowing seeds of faith. One day, He will wipe away every tear, and we will see that nothing given to Him was ever lost.

## A Moment With God

Father, Thank You for being near to the brokenhearted and for seeing every unseen tear. In my grief, remind me of eternity. Help me to fix my eyes on what lasts—to give my life to things that bear fruit beyond this world. Teach me to live not with fear, but with love. Not striving, but surrendering. Not holding on, but giving all. Strengthen me to trust You in the unknown and to rest in the certainty of Your goodness. In Jesus' name, Amen.

## Your Heart's Response

Have an honest conversation with God about your trust—do you believe He sees your pain, that He is near, and that He is working even in the midst of your sorrow? Share your heart with Him, and ask what He wants to whisper to you today.

# Ponder with Jesus

1. What has grief stripped away that you once held tightly? Ask God to help you see what truly matters.

_____

_____

_____

_____

_____

_____

2. How has loss or sorrow changed the way you love others? Invite God to use your pain for His purpose.

_____

_____

_____

_____

_____

_____

3. Where do you need God's comfort today? Sit with Him and let His presence fill the empty spaces.

_____

_____

_____

_____

_____

_____

# Resting in His Righteousness

We look in so many places to fill us up,
And when they don't, we try to hide.
Try to hide from the hard,
The hurt from the rejection and cruelty of this world.
The finiteness that we can't escape.
The evil that glares in our face.
We all naturally hate it
But don't know it corrupts us inside.

So we try harder.
Harder we try to be better.
Or at least better than the comrade
next to us.
For then we feel righteous.
That we're not so far gone.

But there it is again.
It pops up.
Our selfish desires rear their ugly heads.
But we tried so hard.
We gave so much.
We gave so much money.
We gave so much time to those in need,
But why do I still feel so ugly inside?
What is wrong with me?

All I want is peace.
But my relationships are in turmoil.

I've tried and I've tried,
But I'm never good enough.

I hear a soft voice. But I don't know
who it is.

They say, "It's okay. You don't

have to be good enough.
Because He is."

But who is He? What does He know?

He says He was there before the world came into time.
He says He had me in mind.

He said He knew my voice before I cried.
He said He knew my heart before I smiled.
He said He knew the impact He is preparing me for before I even turned 18.
He said He knew every struggle before it took hold of me.
He said He prepared a way before I knew I needed one.
He said His dad sent Him to save me.
He said He never sinned but took on mine.
He said in return He gave me His perfection by dying and trading His life for mine.

He said His name is Jesus. YAHWEH.
My Savior.

Jesus said to me, "I am yours,
and you are mine.
I love you more than anyone."
Jesus said He restored my relationship with our perfect Father, God.
Jesus said I get to live forever with Him.

Jesus said no more striving to be good enough.
For I am good enough for you.
Jesus said His goodness covers me.
Jesus is the perfect One I could not be,
And I am now in right standing with our God Almighty.

Jesus said, "I will continue to give you
everything you need.
Each and every morning.
When you are weak,
I will give you My strength.
When you are tempted,
I will provide a way out,
And when you are faithless,
I will remain faithful."

And that is who He is.
Thank you, Jesus!

## Grace in Focus

No matter how hard we try, we can't make ourselves right with God for our sin is in the way. We strive, we perform, we try to be "good enough"—but it always leaves us feeling empty, exhausted, and defeated for we all fall short of the glory of God. But the gospel meets us right there, in our insufficiency. Jesus did what we never could. He bridged the divide between us and our Father. He lived the perfect life we couldn't live, died the death we deserved, and gave us His right standing with God in exchange for our sin. We don't have to earn it. We simply receive it. And when we feel unworthy, when we're weighed down by guilt, Jesus whispers: "I have clothed you in My righteousness." (Isaiah 61:10 NIV) "Come as you are—I have already made a way." (John 14:6 NIV) "Your past is covered; your future is secure." (Romans 8:1 NIV) This is the beauty of grace: we are no longer measured by our failures or our efforts, but by His perfection. In Him, we are covered, we are redeemed, we are declared right with God. So today, rest in His whisper. Lay down the weight of trying to be enough. You already are—because He is.

## A Moment with God

Lord, thank You for trading Your righteousness for my sin. Thank You for the gospel, which assures me I don't have to strive to be good enough because You already are. Help me to rest in Your grace and live boldly as Your redeemed child. In Jesus' name, Amen.

# Your Heart's Response

Write down three practical ways that knowing you are already in right standing with God—that He has forgiven your past, present, and future—empowers you in your every day life, thank Jesus for this and walk in this freedom each day.

# Ponder with Jesus

1. How do these lies shape the way you see yourself, others, or even God?

_____

_____

_____

_____

_____

_____

2. How does knowing Jesus has already made you whole bring you peace?

_____

_____

_____

_____

_____

_____

3. What is one practical way you can rest in His grace today?

_____

_____

_____

_____

_____

_____

# Your Worth in Him

No one can ever give it to you.
Sometimes it feels like people can take it away,
Or they surely might try.
But it's not theirs to give or theirs to take.
If they try to carry it for you,
It will bruise them and scar you.

You want them to give it to you and prove it to you,
But they can't.
No depth or breadth of words will ever be enough
To fill the never-ending hole inside you.

It feels good for a while and then fades away,
Signaling to your heart to try to get it back.
The heart is desperate.
It wants it badly.
It will do anything—anything—to get it.
But it was never theirs to give.

Your Worth.

It can't be given by those who do not fully comprehend
The value of your beautiful life because they did not create it.
It cannot be given by someone who doesn't know the depths of your soul.
It cannot be given by someone who does not know every hair on your head
And every tear you have shed.

It can only be given by your Creator who knows you better than
you know yourself.
It can only be given by the One who made you.

The One who made no one else even similar to you.

The One who loves you without conditions.

The One who gives His love freely.

The One who proved it by dying for you

While you still were choosing other things over Him.

The One who wants you to feel the immeasurable delight He has in you.

For you are worth it.

You are worth the price of His Son's life.

For that makes you worthy.

Nothing you do, know, or say can take it from you.

God says you are worth it, and that is it.

In stone, unchangeable, forever.

YOU ARE WORTHY

For your worth is in our never-changing, loving God.

## Grace in Focus

The world is relentless in its demands, constantly telling us that our worth is something we must earn. That it's measured by success, approval, beauty, or status. That if we just achieve more, look better, or serve more, then maybe—we'll finally be enough. But the gospel tells a different story. Your worth was never something to achieve—it was something given. Sealed forever in the sacrifice of Jesus. God proved your worth when He sent His Son to die for you—not when you were at your best, but while you were still a sinner. (Romans 5:8 NIV) And in the moments when you feel unseen, when the weight of expectations is too heavy, Jesus whispers: "I made you in love—on purpose." "You are my masterpiece, not a mistake." (Ephesians 2:10 NIV) "I delight in you—just as you are." Your worth is not in your performance. Not in people's approval. Not in anything this world can give or take away. Your worth is rooted in the unchanging love of your Creator. So today, let His whisper drown out the lies. You are seen. You are loved. You are enough—because you are His.

## A Moment with God

Lord, thank You for reminding me that my worth is found in You alone. Thank You for the gospel, which declares my value is sealed by the sacrifice of Jesus. Help me to reject the world's false measures of worth and rest in the truth of Your love and grace. In Jesus' name, Amen.

# Your Heart's Response

Write down areas where you've sought to find your worth outside of God. Take time to reflect on scripture, like Psalm 139:14 or Romans 5:8, that reminds you of your identity in Christ and proclaim your worth to yourself in Jesus name.

_____

_____

_____

_____

_____

_____

_____

_____

_____

_____

_____

_____

_____

_____

_____

_____

_____

_____

_____

_____

_____

# Ponder with Jesus

1. Where have you been searching for your worth, and how has it impacted your heart?

_____

_____

_____

_____

_____

_____

2. How does knowing your worth is secured in Christ change your everyday life?

_____

_____

_____

_____

_____

_____

3. What is one step you can take today to rest and truly walk in the truth of your God-given value?

_____

_____

_____

_____

_____

_____

# Empowered by His Spirit

Like a perfect Father, You have not left us defenseless.
You gave us tools and weapons at our disposal.
You even gave Your own Spirit to us
And put it inside of us.

The same Spirit that rose You from the grave
Is now inside of us who believe!

There is nothing we cannot do.
You have given us every tool to fight each battle.
We have offensive ones and defensive ones.

We have an open line of communication straight to the Almighty God.
We have a book full of YOUR words.
You spoke straight to us.
They carry immense power to change hearts—
To literally mold our hearts more like Yours the more we hear Your words.

For literally every temptation that will fall upon us,
You promise to provide a way out.
Lord, I pray we use Your strength to take the way out.
You are so gracious.

You give us power in the name of Jesus to take lies
And throw them back into the pit of hell where they belong.
Where You are God, there is no fear, shame, or condemnation.

We are free! We are free in You!
You have given us Your power
To defeat every temptation
And every lie in our heads with Your truth.

I believe deep down to the pit of my stomach,
To my tiniest toe,
To the furthest crevice of my brain
And the deepest part of my heart
That I have immense, invaluable, inherited worth in God alone.

I am the beloved daughter of the one true King,
Jesus Christ, my Savior.

## Grace in Focus

The power of the Holy Spirit isn't just an idea—it's a gift that changes everything. The same Spirit that raised Jesus from the dead now lives in you (Romans 8:11 NIV). Let that sink in. You are not powerless. The gospel reminds us that we are not left to fight battles on our own. The Spirit equips us to stand firm against temptation, silence the lies of the enemy, and walk in the victory Jesus already won. And when fear tries to creep in, when shame screams that we are too weak, Jesus whispers a greater truth: "You are not alone—I am within you." "My Spirit gives you strength beyond your own." "Walk boldly—I have already overcome the world." This power isn't just for survival—it's for purpose. It's for living courageously, speaking truth, and stepping into who God made you to be – the masterpiece He made that is uniquely you. In Christ, we are no longer bound by fear, insecurity, or shame. So today, lean into His whisper. Walk in the power that is already yours. The Spirit is alive in you—go and live free.

## A Moment with God

Lord, thank You for the power of Your Spirit within me. Thank You for the gospel, which equips me to live boldly and victoriously. Help me to use the tools You've given me—Your Word, prayer, and Your truth—to walk in freedom and reflect Your glory. In Jesus' name, Amen.

# Your Heart's Response

Reflect on an area in your life where you feel powerless. Pray over it with power in Jesus' name and ask God to help you rely on His Spirit and timing to open doors and overcome. Write down a verse that reminds you of His power and commit to memorizing it this week.

# Ponder with Jesus

1. How does the Holy Spirit equip you to face life's battles?

_____

_____

_____

_____

_____

_____

2. What lies or temptations are you currently battling, and how can God's word help you overcome?

_____

_____

_____

_____

_____

_____

3. What does it look like for you to walk in boldness and freedom today, knowing you're filled with His Spirit?

_____

_____

_____

_____

_____

_____

# The God Who Sees

El Roi—the God who sees.
Our Creator is a God who sees.

He sees you when you're hurting.
He sees you when you feel like you have nothing to offer.
He sees you when you feel defeated.
He sees you when you're lonely,
When you're left out.

He sees you in your darkest moments,
And when you're at your lowest.
He sees you.
And He loves you!

He chooses you.
He chose to love you before you existed.
He knit you together in your mother's womb.
He knows everything about you.
He knows you better than anyone,
For He is the one who made you.

He sees you for you.
And He loves you for exactly how He made you!

He sacrificed His only Son, Jesus, for you.
His perfect Son who came down from heaven in the form of man
To live a perfect life for us.
Jesus let God pour out His wrath onto Him
To pay for everything you've done wrong.

He joyfully traded His perfection for your sin

So you could have a relationship with God.
He paid that price and died for you,
Not after you tried to serve Him as best you could,
Not after you tried to be the best person you could,
But He died for you while you were still sinning,
While you were still choosing things over Him.

While you chose to chase your job, your kids, fun, or friends,
Or that thing that you thought would make you feel satisfied.
Jesus died for you while you were sinning against Him
Because He loves you that much!

He proved there is nothing you have to do to earn His love.
He gives it freely.

Jesus is the only perfect person in our life.
The only one who gives completely without any conditions whatsoever.
He loves you perfectly where you are.

I pray each day you ask God to let you know
And experience just how much He loves you.
It will change your life.

His love fills us up perfectly.
For when we accept Jesus' love,
The hurt of everything else is still there,
But it doesn't have the same grip on us as it used to.
We feel the pain of the hearts of this world,
But we are still full of hope.
Knowing God is working everything out.
God still loves us perfectly.
And we will one day be reunited with Him in heaven,
Where there is only celebrating for eternity.

I pray He opens your eyes to every little way
He is chasing you and showing you His love this week.
He is always pursuing you, I pray you can see it.

## Grace in Focus

El Roi—the God who sees. Not just from a distance, but up close. In every moment, in every struggle, in every place where you feel unseen or forgotten—He is there. (Genesis 16:13 NIV) The gospel is proof that Jesus saw you at your lowest and still chose you. He saw your pain, your sin, your weakness, and He didn't turn away—He moved toward you with mercy. His sacrifice closed the gap between our brokenness and God's perfect love. And when you feel invisible, when you wonder if anyone truly knows or understands, Jesus whispers: "I see you—not just what you do, but who you are." "You are never forgotten—I have called you by name." "My love for you has never wavered, and it never will." Because He sees you, you don't have to hide. You don't have to prove your worth. You are fully known and fully loved—just as you are. So today, lean into His whisper. Rest in the truth that you are seen, cherished, and held by the One who never looks away.

## A Moment with God

Lord, thank You for being El Roi, the God who sees me. Thank You for loving me unconditionally and pursuing me with Your grace. Help me to rest in the truth of Your love and see how You are at work in my life. In Jesus' name, Amen.

# Your Heart's Response

Take a moment to remember the ways God has shown His love to you—even in the smallest details. Write them down and thank Him for His constant faithfulness and care. Ask Him to open your eyes to see His love more clearly, just as He so uniquely sees you.

_____

_____

_____

_____

_____

_____

_____

_____

_____

_____

_____

_____

_____

_____

_____

_____

_____

_____

_____

_____

_____

# Ponder with Jesus

1. How does knowing that God sees you and cares for you deeply change the way you view your circumstances?

_____

_____

_____

_____

_____

_____

2. What does Jesus' sacrifice teach you about His love for you?

_____

_____

_____

_____

_____

_____

3. How can you live today with confidence that you are fully known and fully loved by God?

_____

_____

_____

_____

_____

# Lies vs. God's Truth: Walking in Freedom

Throughout this devotional, we've uncovered the whispers of God's truth—truth that silences the lies we've believed for far too long. Below is a place for you to uncover the lies of the enemy and replace them with Scripture and God's whispers of truth. Use this as a space to return to, reminding yourself of what is real, committing to take every lie captive, and walking in the freedom of God's truth.

| LIES | TRUTH |
| --- | --- |
| | |
| | |
| | |
| | |
| | |
| | |
| | |
| | |
| | |
| | |
| | |
| | |
| | |
| | |
| | |

# Thank You for Walking This Journey

I can't tell you how much it means that you walked through these pages with me.

My prayer is that, in the quiet moments, you heard the whispers of God—reminding you of His love, His truth, and the deep rest found in Jesus. I pray His words settled deep into your heart in a way that changes how you see yourself, your struggles, and the days ahead.

May you walk forward empowered by His Spirit, confident that everything you face in this life can be filtered through and encouraged by the truth of the Gospel. There is no part of your life—no moment too small or too ordinary—where the power of Jesus isn't present, working, and redeeming.

In Him, there is always hope, always strength, and always the promise of new mercies. Even in the everyday, He is your power, your peace, and your purpose.

If this devotional has spoken to you, I would love to hear how God has met you in the midst of it. You can share your story with me on Instagram **@power.of.jesus.in.the.everyday** or email me at **clairefelten@gmail.com**.

Keep listening, keep resting, and keep walking in the freedom Jesus has already won for you.

With love and gratitude,

Claire Staton

www.ingramcontent.com/pod-product-compliance
Lightning Source LLC
Chambersburg PA
CBHW051211120626
46547CB00013B/1307